facing | bereavement

facing | **bereavement**

Edited by
Mark Elsdon-Dew and Ana Lehmann

Alpha International
London

Unless otherwise indicated, biblical quotations are from
the New International Version © 1973, 1978, 1984
by the International Bible Society.
(Inclusive language version 1995, 1996.)

ISBN 1-904074-80-4

Editors' Acknowledgements

*This book depends wholly upon the goodwill of its
contributors who not only agreed to be interviewed
at length, but then checked and re-checked the text.
We are enormously grateful to each of them.*

Published by Alpha International
Holy Trinity Brompton
Brompton Road, London, SW7 1JA

contents

'The eternal God is our hiding place;
he carries us in his arms.'

Deuteronomy 33:27

Introduction

by Jane Oundjian

My mother died when I was 16. She had been ill for a long time. I remember she was on morphine and so wasn't conscious much of the time. She was simply upstairs in her room. When she died, I remember creeping upstairs and peeping through the door feeling that I was doing something wrong. We didn't touch her, speak to her or hold her hand. When the undertakers came to the house, we shut ourselves in the kitchen and listened to music on the radio while she was taken away. I cried briefly at the cremation but don't remember crying again for the next 14 years.

Hopefully that would not happen now. Its consequence was that I was living with a dormant volcano inside me. I thought it was extinct and I had dealt with it, but I hadn't and the eruption came with the next loss.

My husband Nick and I were childless for ten years before we had Jeremy. He was a completely healthy child, thriving and full of beans. When Jeremy was 13 months old, Nick went to India and Pakistan on a month's business trip and I took Jeremy to stay with my best friend in Connecticut, USA. While we were staying there, he caught what we thought was a gastroenteritis bug from a little boy of the same age. The other children in the area all had it and got better. Within a week, Jeremy had died of it. After I had nursed him for two nights, he was taken to hospital and I was persuaded to go home for the night. I did and arrived back at about seven the next morning. It turned out to be about 20 minutes after he had died.

Nobody asked if I'd like to see him and I didn't think to ask – I never saw him again. It was appalling. Whilst nobody said to me he would have lived if I had stayed, I've had guilt about that ever since. I've talked about it endlessly and I don't think it will ever entirely go away, although I have accepted that I did what I felt was best at the time.

We were left with so many questions. I think it's a little easier if you know why someone has died. Either Jeremy was that one in 5,000 who die of gastroenteritis or maybe he picked up some other branch of the virus. The unsatisfying thing for us afterwards was that although tests were done to find out what actually happened, we never got any concrete answers.

My experiences over the deaths of my mother and my son are why I'm so keen on good bereavement care. I found it so curious that for the first weeks after Jeremy died, all I talked about was my mother. My grief over my first loss had lain buried all those years and was the first to need expression.

People on the outside often want to put a time limit on bereavement. About three months after Jeremy died, a family friend came and said that he would like to talk to us. He said that enough was enough and we should be putting our grief away now and getting on with life. I think what he was really saying was that he couldn't cope with any more of it. This I understand. People outside just don't know how to cope. But we shouldn't be saying to bereaved people, 'Enough is enough.' It may be something that takes many years.

Soon after Jeremy's death in 1978 we were visited by the vicar of our village in Sussex and on that day a seed was sown. He spoke to us about the wind of the Spirit in such a way that I began to understand that sometimes things happen that we can't control and that are bigger than we are. When he left I didn't think, 'What was all that about?' I knew I'd been spoken to about something real and true. He'd never met us before and we were not really Christians but he spoke right into our situation and brought us real comfort.

A few years later we ended up at Holy Trinity Brompton in London, enquiring about baptism for our second son, Thomas. Sandy Millar, who was a curate, said to us, 'Do you really want to do it? You've got to remove all the furniture and cook lunch for all the relatives – can you really be bothered?' We thought, 'What a strange vicar!' Then he said, 'Unless of course it's the most important thing you can do for your child…in which case you must find out more about it.' So we did.

I joined a women's group at the church and began to explore Christianity further. I found those verses in the Bible about the wind of the Spirit blowing and we don't know where it's going to carry us. For years I had thought of myself as quite an intelligent person, with a reasonable education, and I had thought that it was an acceptable position to sit on the fence. Then I realised that I was sitting on a place that didn't exist. Because either Christianity is true and therefore incredibly important, or the whole thing is rubbish and therefore not worth anything. I suppose my one prayer was, 'Lord if you're real, then show yourself to me in some way so I can see that this is the way to go.'

It was quite a gradual, creeping thing. I can't pinpoint a day or a moment, like some people can, because I'd never thought I wasn't a Christian. I'd been a nominal Christian all my life, but I realised there was so much more.

Now I look at bereavement – and all suffering – slightly differently. I think that whilst it's not God's will for us to suffer, he can make use of and bring good out of any situation – even the most desperate I believe. How? Because he can transform our response. All of us know people who face hardships in two different ways: they either grumble all the time and say how unfair it is, and why them after all the trouble they've had or they respond in a way that's positive.

In a sense you have to embrace suffering – decide to feel it and get on with it and incorporate it into your experience as something you've got to put up with. It's a part of you. You can never say, 'I'm so glad that happened to me' because who could want such a thing to happen? But you can certainly say, 'I'm so glad I'm not the person that I was when that happened to me.' Because it is sometimes only through hardship and suffering that you grow.

I can't imagine the utter bleakness of not having

the context of a faith. God is faithful and loving –
he doesn't leave you in a bad place. He wants good
things for us, and he certainly wants us to change.
He's into the business of tomorrow really – today
and tomorrow. Changing for the better. I love the
saying, 'Nothing is wasted with God.' You can't
always say that to somebody when they're first
bereaved of course. But you can give them a sense
and a feeling of it. You can hold hope on their behalf.

If I could have seen then what Jeremy's death and
the subsequent path that I've taken developed into,
I'd have been perfectly amazed. I've trained in counselling and sat with people for ten years helping
them with their bereavements.

The stories that follow are different from mine,
but they are about people's responses. Although
they've lost control of the single most important
thing in their lives, which is to keep everybody alive
and well, they haven't lost absolutely everything.
They've still got some control over how they
respond and some of their future is still in their
own hands.

'I was thrown into a pit of despair... Nothing could lift me. I was so, so sad.'

The story of Derek and Francie Lygo

When Derek and Francie Lygo's three-month-old daughter Chloe was a victim of cot death in 1991, their world fell apart. Here Francie, who gave birth to their second daughter Freya in 1993, tells the story of what happened and how a new-found relationship with God has changed both their lives:

I've always been brought up in the Christian tradition. Derek was an atheist but we were married in church. We were engaged within two weeks of meeting each other and it was love at first sight. We still love each other, probably even more than we loved each other then, if that's possible. Ever since I was a child, I have always felt that there would be a time in my life when I would get to know God better. I didn't know when that would be, but I knew it would be sometime. I don't think thoughts like that had ever even occurred to Derek. Life when we were married was going very well: he had a very good job in the City and we were on the crest of a wave. It hadn't always been easy, but we were very, very happy.

Then I became pregnant with Chloe which was the fulfilment of our dreams. We had wanted a baby as soon as we were married. We were thinking of moving into a bigger house, gearing up the mortgage. I did not have an easy pregnancy and I was very ill in hospital for about six weeks before her birth. But Chloe was born and she was a lovely, bouncy, happy baby and everything was wonderful.

Nothing, nothing in the world could have prepared us for what was going to happen next. It was 26 November 1991, in the evening, that she stopped breathing. It was a moment of distraction: Derek was on the phone, I was cooking supper, and when I went to look at her a few minutes later, she was dead. Derek called an ambulance and we attempted to revive her before it came. Eventually it arrived and she was raced to St George's Hospital, Tooting, where she was put in Intensive Care.

It was awful when they were trying to get her heart going. It took a long time, probably about 45 minutes, and a human being dies in three minutes if they don't get oxygen. So that in itself was amazing, that after 45 minutes they were able to start her heart beating again. She was put on a life support machine and never breathed on her own again. She lived another 17 hours, and they were the longest hours in my life. A second seemed like a day, a minute seemed like a year and an hour seemed like eternity. We didn't know what to do with ourselves. There are no words that can describe parents' feelings. She was our life. One minute we had a bouncy, healthy baby, and the next minute the person our whole lives revolved around was dying. Our lives came to a grinding halt. We were unprepared and numb. We wanted to be with her, but the agony of seeing her was almost too much to bear. We were sick with shock and exhausted beyond belief. We had done everything for her in the past, but now we found ourselves helpless and other people had taken over. We could not just pick our baby up, walk out of that place and give her a cuddle which we longed to do. Everything was alien to us and it was a struggle to take it in.

But it was in this situation that the Lord showed his compassion, which was amazing. I had always wanted Chloe christened. Before she became ill Derek was indifferent to it and he hadn't wanted a big fuss, but now he agreed and we decided she had to be christened. Gradually it became obvious that we were going to lose her, and as our hopes for her life faded, we realised it was an ordeal we would have to live through. The chaplain was there and we had her christened. Moments after she was christened I said to Derek, 'The Holy Spirit's here!' – and I didn't know anything about the Holy Spirit. God's love for me was so incredible that he sent his Spirit down to comfort me at that time. I felt this amazing source of strength and peace.

Towards the end our nurse said she thought I should hold Chloe. I was frightened I'd hurt her. Then she said, 'I think she'd far rather be in your arms.' So I did, and she died in my arms. But before that happened, I felt God. I felt overwhelmed with his love and I felt held in his arms, as I was holding Chloe in mine. And the extraordinary thing is that I didn't really know that any of these things could happen. I wasn't a proper Christian at all, apart from going through the traditional motions, and yet that's when I knew that I'd had a physical experience of his love and light. There were tears, but no hysteria. The calmness came from him. I felt I had no right to hold her back, and though my heart was breaking as I held her little hand, I knew with certainty she was with Jesus and that Jesus himself had been longing to hold and care for her.

Then we left the hospital and we came home and we had no child. I was thrown into a pit of despair and my world was black: it was like I was being suspended in a well of black ink. All around there was suffocating blackness. I couldn't look out of a window and feel joy, as part of me had died. Nothing could lift me. I was so, so sad.

We went to Florida for Christmas as had been planned. When we came back, I bumped into Susie Farley, a neighbour I had met at ante-natal classes. Of course I had no baby, and her little baby Harry was there, and she asked where Chloe was and I had to tell her. She was so kind. She was obviously very sad and asked me if I was a Christian. My words to her were that I didn't know if I was, yet all the time I knew I'd experienced his love. Susie asked me if I'd think of going to Alpha, a course at her church, Holy Trinity Brompton. I wouldn't have gone if she hadn't driven me there and introduced me to Deirdre, Lorna and others. But the extraordinary thing was that the moment my foot walked over the threshold of the room there, I felt the same feeling of light and joy and love that I'd felt at the time of Chloe's death.

I never looked back after that moment. That was the only thing that lifted me. I went back again and completed the course. People were so kind. I suddenly knew there was the sky and there were birds in it and there was a rainbow and wonderful things around. There was something worth living for again. Derek couldn't believe the difference in me. He was very suspicious because he thought I was getting involved in some Moonie religious organisation, and he thought he had to stamp it out fast. I managed to persuade him to come on the next evening Alpha course. Very sweetly he said he'd come for me. For the first five weeks he was aggressive and had convincing arguments against becoming a Christian.

Then one day, half way through the course, he was sitting in the barber shop and looking at himself, and he prayed that God would come into his life. He now says that God answered immediately. He says the most amazing feeling was that he felt the whole of the heavens rejoice, as though a voice was saying, 'At long last! We've been waiting all your life for you to do this. Thank you for doing it!'

Our lives changed dramatically after that point. Derek resigned from his job, so we had almost a year together while he was unemployed. The Bible talks about putting you in a spacious place and God did. He gave us the space we needed to be ourselves and to build our faith. He has more than provided for us in every possible way. We've never had to worry about anything. He has also provided us with wonderful friends, far closer than we've ever had before, who pray for all parts of our lives consistently – our home group, my wives' group and other Christian friends. In the same week that our second child, Freya was born, Derek got the job he's in now which is perfect for him. It was such a clear demonstration of God's perfect timing for our lives.

Every day I cry for Chloe. I still love her. Some months after she died I did ask the question, 'Why?' – because she seemed so perfect and it seemed such a waste. You always know when it's God replying because the answer is so amazing. I sensed him say, 'Chloe is much happier in heaven than she would ever have been on earth.'

And I said, 'But I loved her so much, Lord. There was so much that I wanted to teach her, so much I wanted to show her.'

He said to me, 'Now do you understand why you need to love me at least as much as you love Chloe, there is so much I want to teach and show you.'

Little Freya is the most lovely child and we delight in her. As Freya grows up we see how much she would have loved to have had her sister. She adores other children. Grief is not something you 'get over' like a bad cold, and the pain is something you learn to live with. It's the physical missing of the person you love which is the hardest thing to bear. But the Lord continues to be our strength. He has never yet failed. He continues in his Spirit to heal and comfort us, and we always arrive at a restored peacefulness once more. There is no secret to knowing his love, we only have to seek it. Through Chloe's death I knew what 'it' was all about, and that in suffering I was growing up, literally overnight. Growing up is learning to accept God's will. This for me was the moment of reckoning. I felt I had only half lived. My spirit has been awakened, and this was an aspect to my existing on this earth which I had never known before.

The Lord must not only have loved me beyond my understanding, but I think he knew that once I knew and loved him, I would never turn back his power on my life and my family. It has been too strong a force. I will never forget his goodness to me in my darkest hours. I was nothing before him and I would be nothing without him – he is the centre of my life.

Derek and Francie Lygo live in Lincolnshire with their three children (Freya, Sophie and Bertie). They have helped with Alpha courses at their local church where they are members. Francie says, 'We have come a long way since the black pit of despair and grief. God has been constant in his goodness.' She has found two passages from the Bible particularly helpful:

'He reached down from on high and took hold of me; he drew me out of deep waters… He brought me out into a spacious place; he rescued me because he delighted in me.'
(Psalm 18: 16-19)

'The Spirit of the Sovereign Lord is on me, because the Lord has anointed me to preach good news to the poor. He has sent me to bind up the broken-hearted…to comfort all who mourn, and provide for those who grieve in Zion – to bestow on them a crown of beauty instead of ashes, the oil of gladness instead of mourning, and a garment of praise instead of a spirit of despair.'
(Isaiah 61: 1-3)

'I have never felt bereft.'

The story of Zilla Hawkins

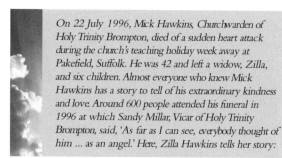

> On 22 July 1996, Mick Hawkins, Churchwarden of
> Holy Trinity Brompton, died of a sudden heart attack
> during the church's teaching holiday week away at
> Pakefield, Suffolk. He was 42 and left a widow, Zilla,
> and six children. Almost everyone who knew Mick
> Hawkins has a story to tell of his extraordinary kindness
> and love. Around 600 people attended his funeral in
> 1996 at which Sandy Millar, Vicar of Holy Trinity
> Brompton, said, 'As far as I can see, everybody thought of
> him ... as an angel.' Here, Zilla Hawkins tells her story:

I was brought up a churchgoer. I had very High
Church parents, particularly my mother, who
had a horror of evangelicals. She died when I was
22. My father was very much a churchgoer, a very
fine man, and he was devastated, not surprisingly, by
my mother's death. By that time, I was living and
working as a secretary in the Lord Chamberlain's
office in London. It deals with all the main royal

ceremonies and occasions, like royal weddings and funerals, and also administers Windsor Castle and Holyroodhouse. It was a fascinating job – great fun. I loved it. I went to church intermittently, but it became more and more intermittent.

Then, at the age of 24, I met Mick. I was sharing a flat with a girlfriend and we had a vacancy for a third person, which we advertised in *The Times*. A man answered the advertisement and we decided to give him the room, which was rather out of the ordinary in those days. People didn't have mixed flats then – it was so long ago! After we told him, the guy said, 'I will move in on Monday and I will bring somebody with me to help me carry my luggage.'

My girlfriend and I decided that we would cook dinner to welcome the new arrival, and we would cook enough for four, and if we liked the look of the 'luggage-carrier', we would invite him to stay as well. He passed the test and that was Mick. That was how we met. His friend continued living with us and became a very good friend. He is Alice's godfather. Then we started going out and got married two and a bit years later. We were very keen to have a churchy wedding at the Queen's Chapel in St James's Palace, where I worked. After we were married, we used to go to church at the Queen's Chapel. We didn't go every Sunday, but we went most weeks, probably more often than not. It was a very conventional service.

When Alice was born in 1979, Mick was very struck by the whole business of birth and new life and this tiny little person who was so perfect. I think he was very blown away by it. He worked in insurance at Lloyd's and two weeks later he was there queuing for an underwriter when he met Gordon Scutt, who ran his own broking firm in Lloyd's. Gordon is an out-and-out evangelist – he doesn't mind what he says to anybody. Mick told him about Alice – I think he said, 'I have just had an amazing experience! I have just had a daughter and can't believe it.' They then talked for about two and a half hours.

Gordon said, 'You must come to St Helen's Bishopsgate with me (a church with a powerful evangelistic ministry among city workers). I will meet you outside the church next Tuesday for the lunchtime service.'

Mick went along as arranged – but Gordon wasn't there. In the end he went in and attended the service by himself. Dick Lucas (Rector of St Helen's) was preaching and he said, 'I wonder why any of you might have come here for the first time today? Perhaps something amazing has happened in your life. Perhaps you have just had a baby or something.'

Mick thought, 'He is talking to me!'

He went the following week to St Helen's and felt that it was speaking to him as well. Soon afterwards he was ill and stayed at home. During that time he read John Stott's book *Basic Christianity*. He is not a reader – he'd only read about five books in his life, I suppose – and so it was pretty amazing. When he had read the book, he got down on his knees and gave his life to God. He was completely full of it all and came and told me, saying, 'I have done the most amazing thing!'

I was furious! I was so angry. I kept saying, 'How can you say you have been converted? We went to church – it is not as if you were a Muslim or something. You can't do this to me.'

I thought he had gone off the rails. He had always been one for great enthusiasms and I thought it was another one of those.

He kept saying to me, 'Read this bit in the Bible…' and 'We have got to go to a different church.' I was very upset because he seemed to have changed. I didn't want to read that bit in the Bible. Somebody, I think it was Gordon, was very wise and said to him, 'Just leave her alone. Don't say anything at all. Just look after her and love her.' And he did.

It is much more difficult to go to church with a baby and so we started going to one around the corner from our home in Clapham – St Luke's in Ramsden Road. The vicar came around to see us and I said, 'My husband says he has just been converted.' He didn't say that he would probably soon get over it, but he did imply it was 'not the sort of thing we do here.'

A couple of months later, Mick brought home a brochure about a Christian house party week away and he said, 'Just thought you might like to look at this.'

I bluntly refused and said, 'I am not going! It says: "Bring your Bible, bring your tennis racket, bring your swimming things." I hate swimming. I hate tennis. Nothing wrong with the Bible.' Anyway, we went. I don't know why.

Mick knew someone called Pippa Gumbel very well from childhood, having been brought up in the same area. So in getting to know Mick I had also got to know Pips and her husband Nicky. This house party week was held in Bedfordshire and Nicky and Pippa were on the host team. Every evening I would come out of supper and there would be Nicky bouncing a football, 'How are you Zilla? Everything all right?'

'No!' I said.

I was used to the Queen's Chapel and robes – and dignity. Yet here there were guitars. Heresy! It was the pits. At the end of the week Nicky and Mick sat me down with David MacInnes (a British evangelist). I said, 'I don't understand it and I don't see why people keep saying that I have to be converted. I hate all this praying aloud.'

He just said, 'That's how they always used to pray in the old days, way back.'

'But I still don't see why I have got to be converted. I am not a Buddhist. I go to church.'

He replied, 'Why don't you go over in ink what has been written down in pencil?' So I said, 'Oh, all right!'

I suppose it was pride by that stage that was stopping me and he gave me the let-out. Within the limits of what I understood at the time, perhaps I was a Christian, but there was so much more. It was not so much like turning around, but more like getting off a bicycle and getting into a sports car. It was that kind of analogy. I realised that if I said I believed in God and he was as amazing as I wanted him to be, then to treat him as anything other than the most important thing in my life was actually wrong. So David prayed with me, thanking God for showing me the way forward and asking him to go with me from now on.

After that, Mick and I started going to Holy Trinity Brompton. It did take a little bit of time for me to get used to the guitars. I like classical music and I love choirs and anthems – but HTB was great.

Nicky and Pippa were running a Bible Study group and I liked them very much. We had asked Pippa to be Alice's godmother. I remember the first time I met Nicky he was so full of life. But it was a horrid ten months, I have to say, from when Mick made that first announcement to me. I feared Mick might have become a loony, and if that had happened it would have been very difficult for the years ahead. But then I became a loony too!

We did an HTB course called Lighthouse. It was a bit more academic than Alpha and we had to write an essay every week on some deep spiritual topic, which was agonising. Mick loved it. It was a super course to do and it lasted a year. Through that we made many more friends. Then we continued to lead groups until we went to Sweden because Mick's job took us out there. I had had three babies by this stage – Alice, Hannah and Martha. I had originally wanted to go, but when we went out to take a look it was very depressing. It is beautiful and clean and the people are civilised. But they are very cold and the weather was incredibly cold. It was the coldest winter since 1942 and the first time that the Baltic Sea had frozen right over. It snowed for five months. I had three young children.

I was pregnant when we went to Sweden and three months after we arrived I gave birth to the baby. He was a breech baby so I was given an emergency Caesarean. When I came round from the anaesthetic, Mick was there. He was in tears and told me we had a boy but he was very ill. That was the first I knew. Later they took me in an ambulance to the hospital where he had been moved, so that I could see him. George lived for ten hours. He had something called Potter's Syndrome which means that he had no kidneys. He never would have survived, but we didn't know that at the time of the birth. He was baptised by the Swedish hospital chaplain. It was quite tough because we had no friends. We had been going to the English church, which was basically dead. People were so sweet but there was no life there at all, and we couldn't find anyone who felt like us. There were one or two. The prenatal care out there is very good and you have your own midwife, who you see every time. She was very sweet and she spoke English.

After I had given birth to George, we went back to see her and she suddenly looked at me and said, 'Can I ask you something?'

I said, 'Yes.'

She said, 'Are you a Christian?'

I said, 'Yes.'

And she replied, 'So am I. I thought you must be.'

It was amazing that God's provision had given me

a Christian midwife. That was very rare. It was an extraordinary confirmation of God's provision and care.

Friends came from England to see us. A friend called Rupert came out the next day. He was a great friend of Mick's through Lloyd's. He was up at Wycliffe Theological College along with Nicky and Pippa at that stage. When he arrived, Rupert told me that he had been to his principal to ask permission to come and Nicky had said, 'Don't worry about the money. I'll organise that.'

Nicky then went to the bank and said, 'I want all the Swiss Francs that you've got.' So Rupert turned up in Sweden with Swiss Francs instead of Swedish Kroner. So in reality he didn't have a bean. I remember laughing and laughing about that.

We felt incredibly supported even though we were miles from anywhere. We never felt abandoned. From the moment Mick told me George was so ill, I was constantly aware of that verse in Genesis about Abraham and Isaac where God says, 'Because you have not withheld your only son, I will bless you.' I really held on to that.

We supported each other and when you have got other children, life has got to go on. That was the mercy of it. If he had been my first, it would have been much worse. The children were very sweet. Everybody was very kind. We were in Sweden for another 18 months. Tilly was born out there, almost exactly a year after George was born. At that stage we were still going to this dead church. The children brought life to the place. They got all these old dears on our side. We were trying to run a group and the vicar would come along from time to time. He would change the subject to something incredibly boring. It was tricky.

In July 1986 we returned to London. Mick's work couldn't find a replacement for him so he had to commute from Sweden for four months. That was a very dreary time. He came back for weekends. We settled back into HTB. It was wonderful to be back. William was born in 1987 and then Rupert was born in 1990. Originally, I had always thought we would have four children. After the end of our Lighthouse course, we were commissioned in the evening service and went up and were prayed for. At the time we had two children, but Nicky came and prayed for us and said laughingly, 'I pray that you bless Mick and Zilla, Lord, and all their six children.' We just felt this was a joke.

After we returned from Sweden, we were at a house party and were asked to tell the story of George and how God had supported us. The next day somebody there came up to me and said, 'I was praying about you this morning and I felt God saying that George wasn't going to be your only son, and that you were going to have another one.'

When I found I was pregnant again I thought, 'It must be a boy.' And it was. It was William. Having had William, we thought that was our six children that Nicky had prayed for. Then we had Rupert. The children have all joined in the life of the church in a big way. They love going to church which is wonderful.

In July 1996 we went to Home Focus (the teaching holiday week in July for HTB's 'family' of churches in Pakefield, Suffolk). It seemed like a normal Focus and Mick just loved it. It was tremendous fun.

We were all there except Alice who was in Borneo doing the World Challenge Expedition – going through the jungle. We arrived and set everything up. Everything was going fine, the weather was great. On the Monday afternoon, Mick, who was a very good squash player, went off to play squash with Nicky. And that was the last I saw of him. I had had absolutely no inkling at all at any stage that there was anything wrong. The first I knew was when Hannah came running up in the chalet. She was in tears.

She said, 'Daddy's had a heart attack.'

I said, 'Don't be silly. Of course he hasn't.'

Then Tricia (administrator of the Focus holiday) came round the corner. She said, 'We have just heard that Mick has been playing squash and has had a heart attack. Will you come?'

Someone said that they would look after Rupert. I just got in the car with Tricia and another friend, Emmy. We drove to the squash club car park and as soon as we drove in I knew what had happened because I saw a police car. Nicky was there in floods of tears. I remember thinking, 'I knew this would happen' – because you hear these stories about people who play squash. And then we went upstairs to the squash club bar and had a glass of water.

The policeman was there and asked, 'Has he been ill at all?'

'No.'

'Have you any idea why this happened?'

'No.'

Then we went back to Pontins. Everybody looked the same. It was so odd that people look exactly the same and your whole life has completely changed in the space of 45 minutes. I just thought, 'What am I going to do?'

I had to tell the children. People found them and they came in one at a time. And then it was a sort of blur really. It was so lovely to be there though. If it had to happen it could not have happened in a

better way. He was all right – there would be no
getting old or getting ill for him. Everybody was
there and was so, so kind. I was totally surrounded
by people who cared and that did feel very like
God's provision. It could have happened two weeks
later when he was due to be going on a bike ride
with Hannah from Land's End to John O'Groats. It
could have happened in the wilds of the Scottish
Highlands with just her. It would have been awful.

There were certain verses that were quite
important at that time. Someone gave me the bit in
Romans: 'Who shall separate us from the love of
Christ?' I put that in the announcement in the
paper. Somebody else gave me three verses out
of 2 Timothy:

*'For I am already being poured out like a drink
offering, and the time has come for my departure. I have
fought the good fight, I have finished the race, I have kept
the faith. Now there is in store for me the crown of right-
eousness, which the Lord, the righteous Judge, will award
to me on that day – and not only to me, but also to all
who have longed for his appearing.'*

It is so beautiful. We were all in floods about it
because it was so right. So that was very special. But
in a funny way what I found so odd and very hard
to handle was that I kept waiting for a particularly
special verse, like the one I had had when George

died. And I didn't feel I had got it. They were wonderful verses, but I didn't feel they were speaking to me in the same way. I felt very much I had got to hang on God's promises, because that was the only thing to do. One promise that bothered me was the one attached to the commandment about honouring our father and mother: 'Honour your father and your mother that your days may be long.' It is the first commandment with a promise. I was really bothered by it because Mick had been amazing to his mother. I thought, 'If God is not going to keep this promise, then why should he keep any of his others?' I saw J. John (a British evangelist) during the holidays and asked him why.

He replied, 'I don't know, but we do know that "all things work together for good for those who love the Lord." ' So I clung on to that verse.

At the time I couldn't see how what happened could possibly be good. I didn't understand how it could be good for me and my children to be left without a husband and a father. I began to feel that perhaps it was because I had always sheltered behind Mick. I had always let him take the lead and do everything and felt relieved that I didn't have to do it – but perhaps through this God was going to make me stand on my own feet and do things in my own right for myself. It would in the end probably be good for me, even if I didn't like it. That has happened now. So therefore it was good even though it was hard.

Sometimes I think for the children that it is a pretty unfair thing to lose your father when you are six and eight. Once again you have to go to God's promise 'He will be a father to the fatherless' and believe it. I think that is the hardest thing. I have just got to believe it even if it doesn't seem possible, because there is nothing else to do. Mick's father had died when he was six. And Mick ended up perfectly normal. It hadn't apparently had any adverse effect on him. So that is an encouragement. He had always had a deep conviction of God's presence.

One thing that people sometimes say to me is, 'He will always be with you. You will always feel him by your side.' That is one of the things I cringe at because he is not. I know where he is. On the whole, it is not something Christians say. On the other hand, I love it when people talk about him and tell me about funny things he did. I don't want to forget him or want other people to forget him. I am aware of people being uncomfortable, but it is much worse for them than it is for me.

Although it is still so immediate to me, it is now history to most people. I don't want people to be manufacturing reasons to talk about him, but I certainly don't want to avoid him in conversation. People were enormously helpful in a practical way in the weeks following Mick's death. One of the most helpful things was when men or boys came and took the boys to play football. I worried about that a lot because Mick used to play a lot with them. For a while I went out onto the Common and tried to kick a football, but then I thought, 'This is not me.' Mick used to take a tennis racket and ball on to the Common and hit enormously high catches for the children. They loved it. But my little lob didn't get anywhere!

The children have been so incredible, particularly the older ones. They have looked after me, rather than the other way around. Alice writes me verses and puts them on my pillow. One of the things I miss so much is the encouragement. Mick was one of the greatest encouragers there ever was. But the children are inheriting it. Occasionally it hits them that Daddy is not going to see them in their school play. He won't be there. And I think it is hard for them when people at school are talking about their parents. They are all so different. Each of them has gone through it on a different plane. There is very much a feeling of being in it together.

We all went to Home Focus the following year. I was convinced that it was vital to go. It is much better to face things than push them under the carpet – all the children agreed about that. Every single moment I am conscious of the fact that Mick is not there. It is not a thing that ever goes out of my mind. Sometimes I get a lurch and it is worse, but it is not something that I am ever unaware of.

I have never felt bereft. I have always felt that God has been very close to me. Sometimes I have found it very hard to read my Bible, but at the same time I haven't felt the hand of accusation. There has just been a closeness. I have never felt anger or bitterness, which is once again part of God's provision. It sounds goody-goody, but I have always felt how fantastically good it is for Mick. I can't wait to be there myself. The month after Mick died, we suddenly got some flowers on the front door step. And it has happened every month since. One half term the doorbell rang and outside there were seven enormous bunches of roses left on the doorstep, named for each one of us but with no indication of who they were from. The card just said, 'Love and Blessings'.

I wasn't aware at first that the flowers always arrived on the 22nd – the day Mick died. But now I have realised that on the 22nd of every month a plant or a bunch of flowers arrives. It is so moving to realise that other people still remember him as being so special. I would love the person to know how very important and special it has been. Now when the children find the flowers on the front door step, they just run in and say, 'It's "Love and Blessings" again.'

Zilla Hawkins has now succeeded her husband as Churchwarden of Holy Trinity Brompton. She and her family are closely involved with many church activities.

'As my wife lay dying, she asked me to promise to go to church...'

The story of Earl Pickens

 A short time before she died, Earl Pickens' wife Donna asked him to promise her one thing: that he would go to Trinity Methodist Church near their Las Vegas home. After her death he kept his promise and visited the church's pastor, who said, 'We've just started an Alpha course. Come along.' This is his story:

My wife Donna and I were High School sweethearts. We married in 1954. We lived in Iowa throughout our married life until I retired in 1994. We had five natural children and we adopted two nephews. Our nephews were Donna's brother's children. There was a divorce in the family, and the year before the divorce, those two came to live with us. The father and mother split and the mother took their two younger children, but she didn't want the two older ones (she was an unusual person). The father couldn't take care of them so we took these two boys, Rodney and Richard.

I worked and travelled a lot. I was in the grocery business, beginning as a stock clerk and ending up as a Senior Vice-President of an Iowa grocery chain. Donna raised the family and I provided the income. During the week I was on the road for most of the time. I travelled 300 to 400 miles from home within the states of Iowa, Minnesota, South Dakota and Nebraska. I must have driven thousands and thousands of miles. We were the type of parents that took the children to Sunday School and picked them up. But then, when our eldest daughter was around 11, Donna said, 'We need to get more involved in the church.'

I said, 'OK. If that's what you want, let's see what we can do.'

So we became pretty faithful churchgoers at St Paul's United Methodist Church at Cherokee, Iowa, where we had our home – and we continued going to church every Sunday up until 1987. In July 1986, we had a telephone call at home from Candy, our eldest daughter. She said, 'I need you.'

She was working as an oncology nurse and lived 120 miles away in Sioux Falls, South Dakota. So we drove straight to Sioux Falls. That was when she sat us down and told us that she had an incurable brain tumour. She was very brave and was more concerned about the two of us than for herself. She passed away in April 1987 and we had a beautiful celebration of her life. She was four days away from her 32nd birthday. After that, we quit going to church. I was angry. I never said to Donna, 'We're not going to church.' I just never made myself available on Sunday mornings and she didn't go either.

After Candy's death, I went back to travelling quite extensively. I think I was trying to hide the pain. And during that time I became an alcoholic. The bottle of Chivas Regal (Scotch) was always in my hand. I never ran around on my wife or did any of that. But it was easy to stay in a motel and have five or six Scotches and go to sleep, wake up the next morning, and try to do my work. I was never a mad drunk. I would drink openly in the house – I didn't hide it – and Donna kept asking me, 'Why don't you quit drinking?'

I wasn't verbally or physically abusive or anything like that, but I'd say, 'Chivas Regal is my right hand.'

I retired in January 1994 and in the interim we had bought a second lake home in Iowa. Throughout this time, I was drinking Scotch every night and I didn't think I could stop – I didn't really want to. I didn't have the willpower. I was still mad.

In 1994 Donna and I had a relationship that I would consider good. It may not have been the greatest, but we got along together. She kept asking me to quit drinking and I wouldn't. Then something happened in June 1994. I had been drinking and she came in and said, 'You've been drinking again?'

And I said, 'Yeah.'

And she said, 'That's it.'

We were at our lake home at that time, and I was working out in the garage where I had a woodworking shop. When the two of us argued, there would often be long periods of silence between us – sometimes lasting for days. But this time I decided to do something. About 30 minutes later I said to myself, 'OK, let's go and face the music.' So I went to find her and I couldn't find her.

Donna didn't drink – but I eventually found her drunk. She was in the water about to fall off a little life raft. If I hadn't found her and she had fallen in, she would have drowned. I jumped in and she said, 'Let me go to the bottom and feel the cool or let the sun burn me.'

I thought she was trying to commit suicide. I eventually found out she wasn't. She read me my pedigree for about four and a half hours – my background and all the things that she knew about me and didn't like about me... I was amazed at the things that came out of her. I hadn't realised how unhappy she was – I'd been blind. Part of it went back to early in our marriage, but most of it was in the last 10 or 15 years. I called our family doctor and he said, 'Bring her in tomorrow and I'll talk to her.'

He was a neighbour as well as our doctor. So I took her to see him the next day, and the only thing he would say was that she wasn't trying to commit suicide. The next day I made a commitment to her that I would not take another drink in my life. And I have never taken another drink. That was in July 1994. We grew closer after that. We travelled – trips to England, Australia, New Zealand, the Caribbean – and we had great fun. We took our family to the Hawaiian Islands three times. When we retired we bought a golfing community home in Phoenix. So we had two homes in Iowa and the third one in Phoenix. We'd winter in Phoenix and then go back to Iowa in the summer. We did that for two years. We were both golfers, but one day Donna said, 'There's something else in this life besides golfing.'

So I said, 'What do you want to do?'

She said, 'Let's go to Las Vegas and see what's there.'

So we went to Las Vegas and found a place that was a golfing community and liked it. We sold our Phoenix home and moved to Las Vegas in 1997. So we would winter there and go back to Iowa in the summer. Las Vegas was a nicer place – we had the golfing and there was activity that wasn't in Phoenix. We liked to go to the casinos every once in a while and Donna loved to play bingo.

One day in 1998 Donna said, 'I want to go to church.'

And I said, 'OK, you find a church and we'll go.'

So she looked in the yellow pages and found Trinity United Methodist Church, which was about eight or nine miles away from our place in Las Vegas. We went to Trinity and liked it and would go about once a month after that.

In November 2000 we were sitting in our family room drinking coffee one morning when Donna started to shake. She said, 'There's something wrong with me.'

I took her to our doctor about four blocks away and he examined her. She was talking and then all at once her eyes went blank and she quit talking. She had a seizure and by the time we got to the hospital she had lost her memory. They did a scan and found it was a brain tumour that had grown to a size that put pressure on her thought processes and body controls. It was just the same kind of tumour as Candy's – a tumour that they could operate on, but they couldn't kill. I was devastated.

Donna had her operation in November 2000 in

Phoenix and they released her to go home on 20 December. We flew her and my daughter back to Iowa. We had our Christmas and then she started taking radiation in January. She was in fairly good form throughout. Through the operation she lost the use of her right leg and arm. So we would move her around in a wheelchair. But we could travel and we returned to Las Vegas for a couple of months. Then we decided we were going to spend the rest of our time back in Iowa around the lake, so that the family could be around her. In July 2001 she asked me one day, 'What are you going to do after I die?'

I said, 'I don't know. I haven't given it any thought.'

A week later she asked me the same question and I said, 'Donna, I don't know, I haven't thought about it.'

A week later she asked me again and I said, 'I really haven't thought about it. I don't think it's time to think about it.'

And she said, 'Well, promise me one thing. After I pass away, when you've got the affairs taken care of, I want you to go back to Las Vegas and Trinity... You may not want to stay there, but be there for the first year.'

I just said, 'Yes.' And that was a promise.

We had a hospice in the area and were able to keep her at home. She passed away at home on 30 September 2001. All the family were with her – 30 of us – and the doctor too. So she said goodbye to the entire family. Whether they were a son-in-law, a daughter-in-law or a child, grandchild, great-grand-child. They were all there. I wasn't mad at God after that. It was different because of her – she made it as easy as possible. When she found out she had a terminal tumour she was mad for about five minutes and then she said, 'My work is over. He's going to take me home.'

By 12 October 2001 I had all our affairs tied up at Cherokee and I drove to Las Vegas, arriving there two days later. I went only because of my promise to Donna. If it had not been for that, I think I would have stayed at Cherokee and gone back to the bottle. But she wanted me to go to Las Vegas and to go to Trinity Church. So as soon as I had got unpacked I called the pastor of the church – Pastor Mike – and went to talk to him. We talked for a couple of hours. Pastor Mike listened to me and said, 'We've just started an Alpha course and I think it would be something that would be beneficial to you.'

He didn't explain what Alpha was, but I said yes. It was the first Alpha course for Trinity and I think there were 36 people there in total. I arrived for their third session and found myself in a small group of 12. We watched the video with a talk by Nicky Gumbel. In my group was a gentleman who had lost his wife four years before, to the same type of tumour. He made a comment about his experience, and then I tried to say something and I fell apart. I kept going back and in one of the subsequent sessions, Nicky told a story about an atheist who fell off the cliff. As he was falling he grabbed a tuft of grass to keep him from falling on to the rocks below. He looked up and said, 'Is there anybody up there who will help me?'

And the voice came down, 'Let go of the grass.'

And he looked up and said, 'Is there anybody else up there?'

That was exactly my position, I reflected, as I sat there. I went home that night, sat on my back patio and had an argument with God for three hours. Finally I said, 'God, it's got to be your way or no way. I give up. I'm yours and I accept Jesus Christ as my Lord and Saviour.'

I hadn't slept or eaten very much for two weeks. I went to bed that night and had my first eight hours of sleep. I had my appetite back the next day. So I called Pastor Mike and went back to church and told him my experience. He prayed with me and everything since that day has been up, up, up... The rest of my Alpha course went tremendously. The retreat day was a very moving, deeply penetrating day for me. People prayed for me. When I started praying, I couldn't finish my prayer...tears have always come easy to me. It was a very deep and emotional weekend for me. After completing that first Alpha course we've had three others and I've been involved in every one of them. I've cooked and been the silent partner in the small discussion groups. It's been a journey of happiness and enjoyment since I've been in Las Vegas at Trinity, and particularly with Alpha.

Before Donna passed away she was reading her Bible, and when she had trouble with vision we got audio tapes for her to listen to the New Testament. I really don't know what I felt about it at that time. I didn't get involved with it personally. Sometimes she'd ask for prayers and I'd pray – but I was never quite sure who to. But now Jesus is everything to me. When I'm missing her, all I have to do is say, 'Jesus, put another patch on my heart.' There will be a feeling come over me of warmth and relaxation, and I know that that patch is warm. My heart is still cracked.

Some people might say that I'm using Christianity as a crutch because of all that I've gone through – but that's not the case. Had my death occurred before Donna's I would have died a death of sin. Now I know that he has a place for me in heaven. Jesus has done so much in my life to change me. God is the focus of my life. I read my Bible – I'm reading Romans right now. Since 30 September

2001 I've probably read the New Testament five or six times completely through. I would never have done that before.

I know that until he calls me home I have a mission of reaching out, touching people, helping carry his word in any way that's his will – not my will. Trinity runs a pre-school with 150 kids, and at four o'clock when school's out, about 35 stay behind until six o'clock when the parents pick them up. I asked the lady who heads that school, 'Do you need a grandpa to help play with the kids?' And she said yes. So I got my police and medical clearance and I play Grandpa Earl to 30-35 kids between four and six every afternoon, Monday to Friday. They're aged from two and a half to about seven – and I play with them. We build blocks, we colour pictures, we sing songs, we read stories. If they're out in the play-ground we play volleyball – whatever it might be. I would never have done that before.

Prayer is an important part of my life today. I pray every day, probably four or five times. I try to pray in the sanctuary 30 minutes before I go to play with the kids at four o'clock. I also work in the church doing 'visitation'. The visitation programme was pretty well dead when I came, and I found out that I could go out and visit people – about five to eight visitation calls a week. I visit people in trouble or at home or in hospital. I call on people that haven't been to church for a year to find out why, and ask them what we can do to help them. We're heading 'Project Recovery' which involves reaching out to all our attendance list – 231 people or families that haven't been in our church this last year. Knocking on the door, taking a gift to them, asking if there is anything we can do to help, if they're still at that address. I would mention Alpha to them – it's a golden opportunity to invite them to Alpha.

My children have noticed the difference. The three oldest daughters were fearful about what was going to happen to Dad in Las Vegas in the land of prostitutes and drinking and sin. It can be like that, but it's no different from any other place in the world. If you seek that type of life, you'll find that type of life. So they came to Las Vegas to see what Dad was doing. And they all went back home knowing that Dad was OK. Now I don't feel I need to stay in Las Vegas any more. What Donna asked me to do has been done. But I feel more comfortable in Trinity Church in Las Vegas than I do in my home church, because of the activities I can get involved with. I'm happiest when I'm doing Christian things – church, working with the little kids, visitation. At Trinity God has led me to get involved with Alpha and reaching out and touching people. That 12 October when I first came to Trinity I knew four people at the church. Today I can call most of them my friends. I think Donna's behind me, pushing!

About six months before she passed away someone gave her a little brooch – a pair of red slippers. The card that came with them said, 'These represent your walk with Jesus Christ – and they're red because of the blood he shed for you.'

It's the only piece of jewellery that I kept and I wear them every day. I always wait until somebody asks me about them, and they're a way for me to express my feelings concerning my walk with Jesus Christ. And she's with me. It was that fifth Alpha talk, with the story about the atheist, that changed everything for me. I wasn't an atheist, but I was off, on, off, on, with God. But that talk really spoke to me by saying, 'Earl, you've got to find your faith or you're gonna hit the rocks.'

And it was when I finally let go of those weeds that were keeping me from falling and said, 'God, I'm yours' that my life started changing.

Earl Pickens attends Trinity United Methodist Church in Las Vegas. He says, 'My relationship with God continues to grow. My prayer time in the early mornings is most meaningful. I find him everywhere I go... It has been a great and growing year.'

'The surgeon came out and said
"I am so sorry, I'm so sorry.
The tumour is of the worst kind."'

The story of Ralph and Cally Crathorne

Christian couple Ralph and Cally Crathorne spoke at Holy Trinity Brompton of how they lived as a family with their young daughter Sasha suffering from cancer – and how they were all with her when she died in 1998. It is a moving story of faith and hope. Here Cally tells the story of what happened:

Nearly six years ago one of my best friends died. She was a truly beautiful person who I had known all her life. She was the sort of person who hummed a lot, had an infectious giggle, and to whom you could chat easily or just as happily be quiet with. We'd go on secret outings together that no-one else knew about. Sometimes we'd just have ice-cream and chocolate for lunch, we'd play 'Barbies' or 'My little Ponies' for hours and it was really good fun. In fact I spent more time with her than I have with anyone else in my life. We knew each other so well and it's strange, we still expect her to appear sometimes and it's a shock when she doesn't. She's left a gaping hole in our lives. She was our daughter Sasha and she was just eight years old when she died.

Sasha was born in 1991. We already had Lucy, who was 18 months when Sasha was born, and we had very normal happy family days. All I ever wanted to be when I was growing up was a mummy, so I was very happy. But from the age of about two, Sasha started to be physically sick, especially in the mornings. We went to the doctor a few times, and because she was growing, they weren't worried at all. Then Polly was born and two weeks later, Sasha fell down the stairs of our little cottage. We took her for an X-ray and in the next few days we noticed there was a change in her. She had lost her balance a bit and we went to the doctor, who said he thought maybe she should have a scan. So on a Wednesday morning I set off for the hospital with Polly, who was four weeks old by that stage. Lucy was at school and Ralph was in bed with male flu, which is what you get when your wife's just had a baby – exhausted. So off we went to the hospital. We went in for an MRI scan and when she came out, the doctors took me into a room and it was just one of those unreal moments... They said, 'We've actually discovered something at the back of her brain about the size of an upside down pear. We think it's probably a brain tumour.'

It is amazing how those words suddenly, in that split second, changed our lives for ever. I rang Ralph, who jumped into the car and followed me, Polly and Sasha in an ambulance to a London hospital where we met a lovely surgeon who said he was going to operate the next day. He said that the surgery would take most of the day and there was a chance that she might not survive, and if she did, she could end up being blind, deaf, or brain damaged. That morning we took her down to the operating theatre and we told her that it would be like Sleeping Beauty – that she'd be put to sleep and we'd wake her with a kiss. Then we gave her our 'special hand squeeze' and we walked away. It was a heart-breaking moment. We knew that nothing would ever be the same.

After leaving her there we went outside and sat in our car, and we prayed something like, 'God, we've got no resources for this and we just turn to you for help. God, we are just collapsing on you and we want you to take our full weight.' We sat there for a long time in the car (for some reason we didn't really have an appropriate place to wait) and the operation took a couple of hours longer than expected. We think that that time during which we prayed and collapsed on God, really set the scene for what has happened in our lives since.

When the operation was over the surgeon came out and he said, 'I am so sorry, I'm so sorry. The tumour is of the worst kind. I'm afraid it's in the wrong place and I may have gone further than perhaps I should have done in trying to get it out. But I'm so sorry, I didn't get it all out.' And behind him stood a man, the anaesthetist, in floods of tears. We were told that the next 24 hours were going to be critical as to whether she would survive or not. There followed a sort of mad ambulance chase to the Intensive Care unit at Guy's Hospital. These Intensive Care units are amazing. They are very intense and organised and calm – and Sasha was there with all the tubes. Her breathing was being aided. After a while, she began to stir a bit. Then a nurse dropped something on the floor and she jumped, so we thought, 'She can hear.' Any little thing was exciting. After a while, she took the mask off her face and shoved her thumb in her mouth. Then she took it out and just said, 'I want my duck,' which is her special cuddly toy. That was another wonderful sign and during the next 24 hours she made an amazing recovery – enough to be moved down to a normal ward.

And there we stayed for a few weeks, with her gradually getting better. Ralph stayed up in London, and Lucy was with us most of the time too. Polly, at four weeks, was shoved under the bed and brought out at feeding and bathing time. Family and friends were amazing with the things they brought. One friend sent flowers every single day. Sasha's was definitely the best bed in the hospital – it smelt wonderful. What people said made a huge difference to us. Some people could bring comfort while others said, well, the platitudes we've all said – things like, 'Children are so resilient' and 'Doctors can do great things these days' and 'What will be will be.' One friend said, 'I had a goddaughter with a brain tumour.'

And I said, 'Oh, how is she?'

She looked at me and said, 'Oh, she died.'

You know how awkward it is in those situations? Those sort of things brought us very little comfort. And yet we had a few friends whose words – sometimes just one small word – would really encourage and comfort us. A clergyman friend was one of the first who came to see us and he said, 'I've been praying in the taxi about what on earth to say to you and I just feel prompted to say to you this one word, which is hope.'

An extraordinary thing about the Christian faith is that sometimes a word from the Bible suddenly sort of comes alive and has this sort of profound effect on your life. Ralph particularly remembers this as one of those moments. He can recall thinking, 'Yes, that's how we're going to live our lives as a family. We're going to live in hope.' Soon after that a Christian friend came and said, 'There is a verse in the Bible I just wanted to remind you of and it's this one from Isaiah that says, "Those that hope in the Lord will renew their strength. They will soar on wings like eagles." ' And so we began to learn this truth together, that this business of hoping was all about hoping in the Lord and not in a particular outcome.

After a few weeks she was well enough to go home and we tried to get back to some sort of normality. She had a special 'line' put in through which you could give her the drugs, take out blood, put in blood – so she was sort of normal. Lucy, who was five, became my 'nurse' assistant. I'd have to scrub up with the gloves and she would open up all these packets with needles, syringes, and bottles – without touching anything that was not sterile. Looking back it seems very strange that I gave her that responsibility, but at the time it was perfectly normal. The doctor decided that because the tumour hadn't completely gone, she needed some chemotherapy. So she was due for a year's chemotherapy, which meant going up to London every third week. Then, the week after the treatment, she wouldn't be at her best.

Sasha was amazing during the chemotherapy. She just sort of carried on. During the year she lost most of her hair and had five blood transfusions. But we had a really happy time and remember it being a really long, good year. It was as if God gave us extra time. At the end of that year, a scan showed that there was still a little bit of tumour left, so they thought radiotherapy would be the thing. That involved ten minutes almost every day for seven weeks. We'd often leave home at 6.30am and we'd burst through the doors in the radiotherapy unit where Sasha would be greeted with her usual morning box of chocolates from the nurses. She'd skip into the unit, into this big dark room where she would be attached to the bed by a clear mask clamped over her head. The lights would go down and she'd have the treatment, after which she would jump down and off we'd go home again.

It could have been a nightmare but it wasn't – it was just a good time. And each step of the way we'd tell the children the latest news of how everything was going, very calmly. None of us seemed to worry because we knew that God was in control. After that, for 18 months, she was absolutely fine. Her hair started growing back and she was very well. Then in September 1996, two and a half years after she was first diagnosed, the routine scan showed that the tumour had come back in a slightly different place. I was absolutely devastated because the doctors had said, 'If she is clear for five years, then her chances of survival are great, but if anything happens within five years, the chances are very slim.'

The next day I read those words from Jeremiah 29:11, ' "For I know the plans I have for you," declares the Lord, "plans to prosper you and not to harm you, plans to give you hope and a future." ' I remember I knelt down and said to myself, 'You know, it's going to be really hard to believe these words as I read them, but I am going to believe them.' So we went back to London and asked more doctors. Was anyone doing anything differently? No, they were all doing the same. Every time we went to these meetings with these doctors, we would pray that we wouldn't ever have to make a choice, because we knew that would be hard to live with. And it was amazing – we didn't have to make a choice. The decisions just happened very easily.

Sasha then had more chemotherapy at Bart's for a few months. By this time I was pregnant with

Jemima, so there was lots of waddling along hospital corridors. In the January of 1997, her immune system got very low. We went into the local hospital for a blood transfusion and it snowed, so we all got stranded in the hospital. We were there for five days in just what we were wearing. Eventually we tried to get home but, a mile from home, we got stuck in snow drifts and the local gamekeeper gave us a lift in his Land Rover. There was a big snow drift across the drive – it was fantastic – and Sasha, having been really ill, with no immunity at all, jumped out of the car in her pyjamas, dashed to the house to put on something warm, then went out into the garden and built an amazing igloo. Her joy in life was amazing to see. When Jemima was born, Sasha helped me. In fact she was a mummy with me, which was a good experience for her to have. Then that summer she had just one more 'direct hit' of radiotherapy, but we really didn't worry about what might or might not happen. In Matthew's Gospel, Jesus says, 'Who of you by worrying can add a single hour to your life?' We really felt that we should not waste time worrying.

Then in the January of that year, another scan showed that the tumours had multiplied and there was nothing more that could be done. The doctors said that it was just a waiting game and that she had probably six to nine months. It was all pretty gloomy so we thought, 'Let's go away on a holiday' – and we decided the only place at that time of the year was the Caribbean. Ralph did a bit of research into it and came home one day and said, 'Great news. I've found a fantastic place on the island of Tobago. The only problem is that there are no flights because there's some cricket match on – and it's incredibly expensive.'

So we thought about it and said to ourselves, 'God likes to give us good things, so we're going to pray about it.' We sat down with the children one morning and prayed for the flights and for £3,500, to make up the difference over and above what we could afford. Then Ralph went off to work.

Later that day he rang up and said, 'Amazing news, we've got the flights – on perfect days.'

And I said, 'Well, I've got amazing news. I opened the post this morning – there were three letters and cheques came out of all of them.'

At that moment in the background I heard a sort of noise and Ralph said, 'Oh, hang on a minute…' and his secretary handed him an envelope which had £500 in cash in it, which had been anonymously posted through the office letterbox. By the time we totted it all up, it was exactly the amount we had prayed for.

We stayed at home for that year. Occasionally Sasha would go to school and during that year, two of her best friends became Christians, and so did her teacher, which was just amazing – all through her. Then, just before Christmas of 1998, she began to go downhill and get a bit more tired and quieter. She spent more time in bed. One day, sitting on the sofa with her, she said to me, 'Am I going to die?'

She had never asked before and I thought, 'I've got to be honest,' so I said, 'Well, the doctors say you will, but we say that God could heal you, but if he doesn't, you will go straight to heaven and we'll be there with you in the blink of an eye.' Then I started crying and she went off and got me some tissues and gave them to me. That was probably our only conversation about that.

She spent more and more time in her bed and in the end she moved into our bed. It was really hard seeing her physical deterioration because she was a very fit-looking child. She was a brilliant dancer and in the last six months she had – with all of us – climbed the six highest peaks in southern Wales. But we carried on praying, we carried on expecting and we sort of moved into the bedroom as a family. Lucy would do her homework sitting there. Polly, who was learning to read at the time, would sometimes sponge her down when she got hot. We tried to make it as normal as possible. We just carried on. Friends and family were amazing, but a lot of the time we just wanted to be us. There was an amazing atmosphere in the house, very peaceful and calm, with nothing sort of panicky about it.

Sasha was amazing. She didn't speak that much towards the end, but when she did, it was to give words of encouragement. I remember once giving her some drugs and I was getting into a bit of a muddle and she said, 'Don't worry, Mummy. I trust you.' Another time I was changing the sheets and I propped her up on the floor. We were just chatting and she said, 'Oh, aren't I lucky to have such a lovely family.' She was only eight years old. We had nurses at home who would come and bring what medicines we needed. Often they did nothing more than take her pulse, if that. They were very good at leaving us on our own. Gradually she stopped being able to get out of bed and she'd just lie very still, very peacefully, listening to songs. We'd read to her sometimes and in the last two weeks she actually went blind. But it didn't seem to bother her. I said, 'Oh Sasha, I don't think you're seeing very well at the moment.'

And she said, 'No, I don't feel like seeing at the moment.' She was just in a very peaceful place.

On the morning of 17 February, we noticed that

things were changing and that there was something different going on with her. So we called one of the nurses who came out, took one look at her, and said, 'Yes, I'm afraid her body's beginning to shut down. Her nose is pinched and her fingers have gone white. There's nothing more – it could be hours, it could be days.'

And we said, 'We're fine, you don't have to stay.' So she went home.

We lay with her and waited really. I remember my hand was on her heart and after a few hours I remember I could feel her heart just gradually… well, the gaps in between the beats were widening. So Ralph put her in my arms and I said, 'Quickly, go and get the girls,' and he ran to get them and they came back just in time. They jumped on the bed and we were all holding her and they were there for her last breath. It suddenly went very quiet and I remember there were hailstones on the window – it was most extraordinary. It was almost one minute she was there and the next minute… It was like a physical going – I could almost see her going. We were left with her body, and her spirit (or her soul) just went.

We looked at each other and we were so shocked, because we didn't expect her to go. We couldn't believe it. We all just cried and cried and then we laughed and then we cried. It was extraordinary. After a while we lay her on the bed and the girls went to get mattresses and lay down on the floor. We all lay next to her, holding her hand, and just went to sleep for a couple of hours. It was so peaceful. Her body looked so beautiful in the half hour after she died. Her face was extraordinary. She looked young, she looked old, she looked sort of ageless.

The next morning we prepared her body, which I'd actually read about. It is very simple and we wanted to do it ourselves. We dressed her and then Ralph carried her to the spare room, where we thought it would be best to put her body. We somehow decided we were going to keep her body at home until we took her to the church (which you can do – there's no law about it). So we lay her body out surrounded by flowers and it seemed to be very helpful for people to see that she'd gone. It was just her beautiful body that we were burying and not her. The girls were amazing. They'd invite people in and say, 'Hi, do you want to come and see Sasha?' Some people would sort of go, 'Oooh,' but the girls would say, 'No, no, just her body.' It was all very natural and it helped a lot of people – it really did. I knew where she was and knew that God was suffering with us too. We didn't feel guilty or panicky – we were just absolutely heartbroken.

Eight years doesn't really seem long enough to live, but for her it was a complete life.

We decided to organise her funeral ourselves. We rang the undertakers who delivered a coffin. The most difficult thing was putting the lid on for the last time. We kept opening it, having a look… But in the end we had to put it on, and that was a really difficult moment. Then we put her in our car and took her to the church ourselves. It was a real DIY funeral and it was amazing. It was incredibly sad, but a very joyful, uplifting occasion. Hundreds of people came. I don't know hundreds of people, but she did and they came from all over the place. One friend flew from America just for the day. Then after the service, we put her in our car again and drove her off to a graveyard near our house. We had a very simple burial where people prayed what they wanted to pray. Then we all put earth in – all our friends and family helped bury her.

The next few weeks were really a blur. I don't remember them much and we just had to get on with learning to be sort of normal again. Lucy went back to school, Polly stayed behind, Jemima was still only two years old. We missed her so much and we cried a lot, all at different times. Often little things would trigger us off, but we were very open. We'd cry when we wanted to, in front of people. A lot of crying was done and it really helped. I found the first two years very hard and now, nearly six years on, it's still incredibly painful but the edge has been taken off a bit, with time. We haven't got over it because I think some things you never get over. I find the anniversary of her death, her birthday and Christmas very difficult.

We've had to cope with people's reactions to her dying. I remember one lady at the check-out in Sainsbury's who knew me and Sasha very well. I met her there just after the funeral and she said, 'How's your daughter?'

I said, 'She died a few weeks ago.'

And she said, 'Oh, I'm so sorry, I know just how you feel. My dog died last week.' I remembered she had no children and that her dogs were her life, so I had to sympathise with her.

I found it really hard seeking God to begin with, but I knew he was there, waiting for me. I knew God knew exactly how I felt and he'd be patient. Our children have been amazing. They're full of faith and pray endlessly for people to get healed, but of course they're very sad at times. We've found it unhelpful asking the question, 'Why?' because there's no answer. It doesn't help. I do know that her life wasn't a wasted life and, as parents, I think Ralph and I were really privileged to see her whole life from the beginning right through to the end. I'm very grateful for that.

'We still trust God.'

Ralph Crathorne

People ask, 'Were you praying for healing?' – and, given the outcome, 'Was it worth praying for healing?' But for us this was all part of trusting God. We know that it's in the character of God to heal and to make whole and so, yes, we did expect him to heal Sasha. That is how we lived those years – expecting him to do that. But the other part of trusting God is saying, 'We're going to go on trusting you even if you don't do what we expect. And if that happens, our dreams may be shattered but our hope in you is going to keep going.' We often pray in this way as a family: we say, 'Lord, we believe you can do this, because you're God. What's more, we're expecting you to do this, because we think it would be just like you. But if we're wrong that doesn't matter, because we're still going to trust you because we know that you love us, and that one day we're going to be with you.'

Sasha loved being prayed for – but she also loved praying too. I remember when she was about six years old, we went to pray for a friend in her mid-60s called Cindy, who was in the last stages of cancer. Sasha prayed, 'Lord, will you heal Cindy,' and then she said, 'but I don't mind if you don't, because then she'll get to be with you and Jesus.'

Ralph and Cally Crathorne continue to live in Kent where they attend their local church with their three daughters.

Facing Bereavement

by Jane Oundjian

Coming to terms with the loss

Bereavement is perceived by many people to be a kind of journey. Most people would agree that in the beginning you're in a state of great shock. You might be feeling numb and totally unbelieving of what's happened. You have been catapulted unwillingly into this new place and you are without a route map. The world outside seems to go on oblivious to the fact that this momentous thing has just happened to you. Soon after of course events take over, because there's such a lot to do in the first week or two after someone has died. There's the funeral, the family and all the arrangements. So it's a very busy time and there are a lot of people about. Whilst you may be feeling terrible, it is a time when there's plenty of activity which concerns the care and wishes of the dead person. So you're still very much connected to them, because everything is about them.

So I think the first real black hole for most people comes when the funeral service is over and all the fuss has died down and everybody's gone away. You go home that day and shut the front door and the person's no longer there. You're left with the rest of your life spreading out in front of you, and a house full of memories and perhaps possessions belonging to the person you love and miss. So what on earth do you do? I think that really is the first 'big stage' if you like.

Saying goodbye

People die in different circumstances. I have a lot of people who come on the Bereavement and Loss course whose loved ones have died of a terminal illness like cancer. It's been terrible, but all the goodbyes have been done. It has been gradual and things have been prepared and the funeral's been discussed – so in some ways there's been a good ending.

Then you have the person whose car went into the back of a lorry or who has had some other sort of terrible accident or a heart attack at the end of the garden – so everything's unresolved and there are no goodbyes. In these kind of cases I encourage people to think about going to see the body and saying their goodbyes to their loved one. They very rarely seem to regret it but find it a tremendous help in accepting what has happened. Sometimes people make more than one visit, and although undertakers may moan about the inconvenience, I say to people, 'This is your special time and opportunity to do what you need to do.'

Likewise it is important to realise that the funeral service, however lavish or however private, is principally for the family of the person who has died and they can choose to do it more or less any way they want. We tend to go along with whatever doctors, undertakers, vicars, etc, advise us to do, but actually people are quite free to make their own decisions. You may not want the body embalmed, although embalming is the norm. You may want to keep the body at home, although most go straight to the morgue. You may want to decorate a bio-degradable coffin or play Jimi Hendrix in church. So I encourage people not to be afraid of finding out if what they and their family want is possible.

If the death has been sudden you can still do quite a bit about trying to make an ending. People sometimes go and visit a place where something happened, some months later perhaps. Or they might write their feelings down or write a goodbye and do something special with the letter. We all need some sort of closure to be able to move forward.

Coping with life on the outside

I think it's terribly important for people when they're grieving to keep control of their own lives as much as possible, and not feel that they ought to be doing or not doing things. If someone invites you to something you should be able to say, 'I'd love to come, but if I can't face it, could I tell you on the day that I'm not coming?' So I suggest to people not to tie themselves down with making decisions – because they're in this unpredictable state. Feelings and reactions are all over the place – anything triggers us off so we cry or go downhill or feel a little better. You just don't know how you're going to be at any given moment – how you're going to be sleeping, whether you're going to be eating properly, how you're going to be feeling. You may be very tired, because grieving's an exhausting process and you are trying to live life on the outside with all this turmoil and pain going on inside.

I would say, 'Try and get your family and friends to accept a bit of flexibility – that sometimes you might want to do things and sometimes you might not, and could they please ask again if you say no?'

Some people make themselves extra busy when they're grieving, because they hate being at home. So they throw themselves into work or into social activity. But other people just withdraw from everything and shut the door and like to be alone. It's very varied and people need to find what suits them best – bearing in mind that if you do turn to a lot of frenzied activity, there will come a day probably after some months or even a year, where you'll realise that you are ready to be less busy and a bit more reflective about your loss, and probably willing to spend more time at home quietly.

Relationships with other people

The response of those close to you when you are bereaved can be quite surprising. In my experience most people have friends who they think will be there for them, and they are quite shocked when some of their friends seem to take a couple of steps back and fail to keep in touch. After some time we may realise that our friends weren't really equipped to help us, or were afraid of death or didn't know quite what to do. We find that other people come forward – unexpected people who perhaps we don't know so well – who are extraordinarily understanding and helpful. So there'll be some surprises in store. It's not about whether your friend likes you as a friend or not. It's just there are a lot of people in our culture who are not comfortable with death and dying and illness, and really have to move back from it (usually because they've got their own fears and unresolved feelings about a previous loss or something). So we shouldn't feel hurt. Instead we can begin to identify who the people are who can cope and we can talk to, and that's our support group. It won't necessarily be our closest group of mates, it might be somebody else.

Many people have to go back to work very quickly – and the workplace may respond in many different ways. Some bosses will let you take as much time as you want, others will say, 'You can have off till the end of the week. We'll see you back here on Monday...' It seems to be very varied. When at work we will have to take responsibility for what we tell and to whom – which colleagues we want to tell what has happened.

We also need to be prepared for the awkward questions after a death, like 'Where do your parents live?' or 'How many children have you got?' or 'What does your husband do?' – innocent, throwaway questions at social occasions. If we've lost somebody – a father or child – we've got to decide whether we want to give the real answer, or whether we want to skim over it. But we must try not to be taken up short by such an innocent question. If we decide the person we're talking to is a really nice, sympathetic person and we like them, we may want to say, 'Well actually I did have five children, but one of my sons died a month ago…' But then we've got to be prepared to rescue them, because we know what's coming, but they don't, and they're going to feel awful.

So in a strange sort of way we've got to take some charge of our environment and our relationships, which might seem rather unfair, but it will help things to run more smoothly for us and give us a little more control.

Belongings

I think the timing about what to do with belongings and clothes is a very personal matter. I've sat with widows in the counselling room who have had to get rid of every piece of clothing within a week. One elderly lady once said, 'I had to make that bedroom my bedroom.' Another person might see me and say, 'I'll give one or two bits away, month by month, and find somebody to give them to. But now they belong in the room with me.' People's needs are all different. We shouldn't be persuaded by other people to give things away too quickly. I gave away all of Jeremy's toys within a week, because I thought that by giving them away, I'd be giving away the pain of having them. But about three months later I wanted them desperately. My wonderful sister, who I'd asked to give them to a children's home, said, 'Don't worry – they're all in my attic.' She'd kept everything because she was much wiser than I was and she knew.

I know of a lady whose teenage daughter had died and she slept with her daughter's sweatshirt. She said, 'I think I'm going mad – I sleep with her sweatshirt.' Of course she wasn't going mad. It simply allowed her to feel close to her daughter. But after a period of time she stopped sleeping with the sweatshirt. On the other hand, when people are seriously stuck there is usually something very obviously wrong. If you're laying a place at table for somebody who died 20 years ago, there's clearly a bit of a problem. But other things that we do – like holding on to possessions – well, it's whatever helps you to get through the day really.

Avoiding the pain of grieving

There are lots of ways of not grieving. Some we may do consciously, others unconsciously. I suppose the most obvious is when people take to drugs, alcohol or addictive medicines in an unhealthy way. Anti-depressants are fine when prescribed by a doctor and used as they should be. But if somebody's taking a cocktail of alcoholic drinks and anti-depressants, it will suppress their grieving for as long as they go on like that. Sometimes people try to avoid their pain by over-activity, by restless travelling or by moving house. Quite often people will say, 'We're going to move away from this town because this is where it happened,' and then they're surprised when their pain goes with them and they wish they were back in familiar surroundings. Our pain goes with us wherever we go. I had an uncle whose wife died and he moved to three European countries, trying to settle, but he couldn't settle anywhere because he took his sadness with him to all those unfamiliar places. Eventually he came home.

Heightened busyness or work activity, deciding not to talk about it but just to get on with life, or 'keeping the lid' on our feelings, are all ways of delaying or avoiding the pain of grief. Sometimes this can be a perfectly good tactic as it allows us to cope with our necessary daily life. But at some stage the bereaved person will probably realise that the moment has come to take some time to look at their loss and the feelings around it.

Grieving is about being sad really – being prepared to be sad and to face whatever it is that we've lost. It is very possible to run away because it's going to be painful. But sometimes if you turn and face the loss, it's not quite so bad to face it as you expect. Grieving is allowing your feelings, your thoughts and your emotions to come over you in waves, and to accept that you'll have days when you're a bit better and days when you're a bit worse. It is taking time to allow yourself to think things through, to try to work out who you are now this person has gone. The 'stiff upper lip' is OK if you have to use it for certain reasons. But if you use it endlessly (like I did over my mother), it becomes a way of life and you're just sitting on a volcano. Of course we can't always allow ourselves to let go or collapse because we've got responsibilities, or we're in a very difficult life-stage, or we've got decisions to make. So defence mechanisms are healthy up to the point that they allow us to get by and to cope. But they're not going to be the long-term solution.

Families

You'd think it would be the most marvellous thing to be able to grieve with your family and in the beginning people always say, 'It's fantastic because we've got our family, we've got each other.' But as the days and weeks go by, it doesn't always work out like that.

I often sit with people who've lost perhaps a parent – a mother for example – and you'd think it would be easy for them to go home at weekends and talk to their father, but it's not. Either the son or daughter breaks down all the time, or the father breaks down, or neither of them dare to say anything because they are trying to protect one another. Each family member is actually grieving a different loss with different sets of feelings. People can start to feel very isolated even within a family setting.

I think people should persevere with trying to communicate feelings and with using the deceased person's name and talking about them often. People say, 'I go home and no one mentions Mum's name' and that's so hard, because everybody's aware of this figure in the room who's never mentioned. So for example, if someone is visiting their father, they might try and say something like, 'Gosh Dad, wouldn't Mum have loved this?' He'll either murmur some response but not want to talk about it, or he may pick it up and be prepared to open up a little. You're giving people openings really, which I think can be very helpful.

Men and women often grieve very differently. The generalisation would be that men are much more 'doing' based – so they'll try to solve problems, sort things out, get on and move into a new life without the person. They'll often have lots of feelings – but unexpressed. Whereas women generally are much more into experiencing the feelings and not so much in a hurry to get on with the 'doing'.

Children

Children need to be kept in the loop – they need to know what's going on, to be involved, given the opportunity to go to the funeral or contribute something. They need to know how people have died. Having secrets in families is something that often happens, because they'd rather the children didn't know everything. But it is better to keep children informed, at the right sort of level of information for their age, about something that's true and that can be further explained as they grow up.

There are lots of wonderful materials for bereaved children. There are games, picture books, drawing books, story books – all dealing with the subject of death and dying. They allow a child to be colouring or drawing or doing a game, so they have their attention on that, and they're talking while they're doing it. I'd encourage painting, clay, or anything where you can let the child become absorbed and then talk to them a bit about the person who's gone. I think it's really important for them to have an opportunity to express their emotions, but we shouldn't be surprised if they suddenly switch off and start talking about something really trivial. They'll be very sad one minute and then they'll suddenly rush off and roar with laughter and have a wonderful time the next.

Children can't stay with difficult or sad feelings for a long time – they're not able to do that. You know when they don't want to do any more because suddenly they're up and off and they've finished with it. It's not that they're not understanding how dreadful everything is, it's that they've done all they can for now. We might come back to it with another story tomorrow, so we can follow their lead. But we need to be as truthful as we can with them.

Practical help

When somebody very close to us dies, quite often we've got new tasks and things we have to do. It may be that we've got to take on all the family paperwork and bills which we've never done before; it may be that we have to begin cooking and looking after the family when we've always been out at an office job before. If we're getting overwhelmed, we should try and ask for help and advice and input.

Many people want to help you when you're bereaved, but they don't really know what to offer. People often say, 'If you need anything, call me' and then we never call, because that's just the way our culture is. The trouble is we often don't feel strong enough to ask for help. It is good to remember what things would be really helpful so that if someone asks we can immediately say what we need. Some of the things that have been offered in my experience are:

- *someone coming in to help you open all those brown envelopes and deal with paying the bills*

- *someone coming in to do a pile of ironing*

- *someone helping with cooking*

- *someone to drive/accompany you to do something difficult*

- *someone to help with babysitting.*

So we need to try to think practically about what could be a help. People should not necessarily expect to be able to do everything themselves – they're not 100 per cent and they're missing their loved one. I would say, 'Don't set such high standards for everything as you did before. You won't be able to meet those standards just at the moment. Give yourself a break at regular intervals and some little treats and if possible plenty of rest.'

Faith in adversity

It seems to me that there are lots of extra questions after someone has died for people with a Christian faith. In the very beginning it can almost be more difficult for a Christian. The kind of questions that come up are: ' If God is all powerful, how could he let this happen?', 'How can God be a loving God?', 'Can my faith survive this?', 'Is this a test?' Sometimes in Christian circles a trite answer can be given by someone well-meaning, like: 'God doesn't make mistakes' or 'I'm sure God has a purpose in this.' This kind of answer is of course true on one level and may be given in kindness, but actually conveys that the person doesn't understand the agony of the original question. Difficult questions have to be asked but they cannot humanly be answered. We need people who will get along side us while we struggle with understanding God's purpose for us.

But some people's faith isn't shaken at all – they know it's terrible, but their faith can encompass it. A vicar I know once said, 'We need to be a Good Friday people, living on Easter Sunday' – and I think that's wonderful. We've got to be able to live in the mess of Good Friday, but grasp Easter Sunday with our minds.

The Bible of course is full of people angry with God. You've only got to read some of the Psalms or David's Lament in 2 Samuel 1. But God can cope with men and women being angry at him. He'll cope with it and turn his face towards us. Anger as a way of life is not what I mean here, but the anger in these stages of terrible loss is about fear and disappointment and rejection and loneliness. Anger that cannot be expressed may end up going inwards as a sort of depression. There's a lot of anger around when people die – the more violent the death (for example a suicide or an accident), the more angry feelings there seem to be.

One very big question that concerns some bereaved people is whether the deceased person has gone to heaven. The first thing I would say is, we don't know for sure the state of anyone else's heart, right up to the last moment when they die. We think we're sure about people because we've known them for a long time, but I believe we never know the situation of another man's soul and inner heart.

We must never forget the parable of the workers in the vineyard in Matthew 20. The man paying the workers says, 'I want to give the man who was hired last the same as I gave you.' God gives us that chance for the full reward right up to the last minute. Remember also Jesus on the cross with the two thieves either side of him. One of them calls out to Jesus, 'Lord...'. And Jesus says, 'Tomorrow you will be with me in heaven.'

So people really do have until the very last moment to get right with God. I think that is what he wants for them because he is a generous God. Also we know that God is absolutely fair and always does the right thing and that we can never be more fair than he is.

Spiritual support

There's a wonderful line in an article written by Nigel McCulloch, the Bishop of Wakefield, which says, 'Christ has no hands on earth but yours.' So our Christian friends have the physical hands to bring us comfort. So we can seek them out, ask them for help, join a home group, or find someone to pray with on a regular basis.

If we feel we've been let down by God and our faith is very weak, we can say to one or two of our friends, 'I can't pray at all at the moment – would you pray with me or for me?' We might be able to say to God, 'I can't pray to you... but Marion and Jane want to pray for me, and that's my act of prayer to you at the moment, because I can't do any more.' I think asking others to pray for us when we can't is really important.

Some people may find, on the other hand, that although things are desperately sad they are feeling extraordinarily close to God – what a clergyman friend of mine called the 'glimpses of glory' piercing the engulfing blackness. They will still need their Christian friends however, to laugh and cry with, to be alongside them on their journey.

Sometimes facing going back to one's regular church can be really difficult, because everybody knows what's happened and there's a worry that we're going to cry. It's really hard. So I recommend to people going to church with a friend who can sit with them and take care of them. You don't need to be doing extra well just because you are a Christian. The pain is the same. Christians need time to be able to grieve without having their faith challenged from the outside.

How can I help?

For those who know someone who has been bereaved

When you know someone who has been bereaved, do write them a letter. People often feel inhibited about this. 'I'd like to write,' they think, 'but I didn't know them very well,' or 'I'm not quite sure what I would say.' But do write anyway. I frequently hear people say, 'The letters are so wonderful and I've kept them and I read them over again and again,' or 'I didn't know that so many people thought so much of him.' Likewise if you see the bereaved person unexpectedly somewhere, do go up to them. We don't have to know the 'right thing' to say, but a touch on the arm, a smile, even tears, mean so much. Don't avoid mentioning the person who has died. They will probably be so relieved that you have done so. By saying something like, 'I often think of John...' you immediately unlock something and you have shown your willingness to talk about him if they want to. If they don't pick up the lead, don't worry or feel rejected. They will remember that you were willing and they may talk to you in the future.

People sometimes need a lot of practical help – washing, ironing, cooking, babysitting, driving, shopping (going into places to buy food is daunting if you're in the first stages of grief). You could say, 'Couldn't I come in one day and do a bit of your ironing for you?' It's a huge help. If you know somebody who's recently been bereaved, the most marvellous thing to do for them is to cook them something and take it round – it's a lovely thing to receive and it's nourishment for the body and the soul. If you know a bereaved parent who never gets out, how wonderful if you could say, 'Look, I'd just love you to go out for the evening. So why don't I come over and look after your children?' Try to think practically about what could be a help. They may want you to do something a few times and then suddenly, the fourth time, they say, 'No thank you' and you may wonder if you shouldn't have offered. You just need to take a deep breath and realise that it was the wrong moment. Try not to be too timid to go back again a week later and ask how it's going. We've got to bury our sensitivity. If people are having a bad day they might be quite abrupt, but they might welcome us with open arms tomorrow.

In the early days and weeks after the death there will probably be quite a few friends getting in touch with the bereaved person, but as the weeks turn to months people fall away and forget to stay in touch. So keeping in touch in the longer term is something very positive that we can do for others. A phone call, a text, a visit, an email – there are so many ways to let someone know that we have not forgotten. It is helpful if we can accept the way that our bereaved friend or relative is feeling and are able to cope with their sadness. Telling someone that 'your mother wouldn't want you to cry' doesn't really meet them at their point of need. Often it is a question of just being with them – sitting with them, crying with them. There is no need to feel you have to make it better, just share in their sadness for a while. As time goes on we will be able to suggest an outing or a meal and they will slowly feel like doing more and seeing more people. One last very helpful thing is to make a mental note of significant dates such as birthdays and anniversaries, and to make sure to remember the bereaved person at Christmas and on Bank Holidays or any other special date in the calendar. Also make sure that they too have remembered and made a bit of a plan for that day. I have known someone build up courage to go to church shortly after her mother's death, only to walk in and find that it was Mothering Sunday and she hadn't realised! Basically it's all about common sense, spontaneity and kindness. It takes a little effort but it might make all the difference for your grieving friend.

When does grief end?

It is curious that although death is universal, the one certainty apart from birth, we are so unfamiliar with it and with the course of the grieving process. People often ask 'When will I finish?' when talking about their grief. In one sense we will never finish because that loss is always with us. However we can expect in a very real and tangible way to experience significant recovery from the debilitating effects of mourning. It's just that the time this takes will vary hugely from person to person, and we need to take our eyes off other people and their progress and concentrate on our own pace of recovery.

Sometimes people can feel very stuck over one aspect of their grieving, or very isolated or unable to express all their varying emotions. In such cases I always recommend trying to do something proactive. Joining a bereavement group or seeking some bereavement counselling can be a great help.

However, finding an outlet such as writing, painting or pottery, or taking up a sport can also be really helpful in dealing with those deep felt emotions.

If life seems to stop at the time of a death, then the end of grieving will be marked by a sense that life needs to move on once more. We will begin to have renewed interest in the world outside, following the news, going to the cinema, socialising with our friends. Physical symptoms such as aches and pains, sleeplessness, lack of appetite and our general sense of fatigue will diminish. We will have less trouble with difficult emotions such as anger and guilt. When we think of our loved one there will no longer be acute pain, rather a lingering sadness.

Our aim is not to return to the state that we were in before the death. That can never be. We will have gone through so much change over the months and years. However we will probably acknowledge that some of these changes are for the better. Suffering has a way of bringing wisdom, maturity and a shift in what we value in our lives. Our task is to find a place for our grief within ourselves, to assimilate it and the emotional legacy of the person we loved and lost. Thus we can, as it were, carry them with us wherever we go. We do not give up the relationship but we internalise it and realise that it is secure and cannot be taken from us ever again.